D0643520

FANTASY HOCKEY MATH

USING STATS TO SCORE BIG IN YOUR LEAGUE

BY SHANE FREDERICK

CAPSTONE PRESS
a capstone imprint

Sports Illustrated Kids Fantasy Sports Math is published by Capstone Press,
1710 Roe Crest Drive, North Mankato, Minnesota 56003.
www.mycapstone.com

Library of Congress Cataloging-in-Publication Data
Names: Frederick, Shane.
Title: Fantasy hockey math : using stats to score big in your league / by Shane Frederick.
Description: Mankato, Minnesota : Capstone Press, [2017] | Series: Sports Illustrated Kids.
  Fantasy Sports Math | Includes bibliographical references, webography and index. |
  Audience: Ages: 8-12. | Audience: Grades: 4 to 6. | Description based on print version
  record and CIP data provided by publisher; resource not viewed.
Identifiers: LCCN 2015050656 (print) | LCCN 2015049418 (ebook) | ISBN 9781515721727
  (eBook PDF) | ISBN 9781515721598 (library binding)
Subjects: LCSH: Fantasy hockey (Game)—Mathematical models—Juvenile literature.
Classification: LCC GV1202.F345 (print) | LCC GV1202.F345 F74 2015 (ebook) | DDC 793—dc23
LC record available at http://lccn.loc.gov/2015050656

Summary: Describes how to use statistics and math to create and run a successful fantasy hockey team.

Editorial Credits
Aaron Sautter, editor; Sarah Bennett, designer; Eric Gohl, media researcher;
Katy LaVigne, production specialist

Photo Credits
Newscom: Cal Sport Media/Del Mecum, 27, Cal Sport Media/Mike Wulf, 28—29, Cal Sport Media/Scott
D Stivason, 25, Icon Sportswire/John Cordes, 11, USA Today Sports/Marilyn Indahl, 4—5; Shutterstock:
albund, 2—3; Sports Illustrated: Damian Strohmeyer, cover, 20, David E. Klutho, 8, 9, 10, 14—15, 16—17,
21, 22—23, Robert Beck, 24, Simon Bruty, 6—7, 18—19, 26, Tony Triolo, 12—13

Design Elements: Shutterstock

Printed and bound in the United States of America.
009678F16

TABLE OF CONTENTS

SCORING A WIN!

In 2015 the Minnesota Wild opened their season with a thrilling comeback win. Zach Parise scored a **hat trick** to help his team to victory. But Parise didn't just help the Wild win. Parise's three goals helped many fantasy hockey players find victory too.

You don't need to be a gritty player like Parise to win at fantasy hockey. Knowing about the National Hockey League's (NHL's) teams and players is a good way to start. But to build a championship fantasy team, you need to dig into the **statistics** of the game. You need to know how to use the numbers to your advantage. Learn to do the math, and soon you'll be running your own unbeatable fantasy hockey team.

hat trick—when a hockey player scores three goals in a single game

statistics—numbers, facts, or other data collected about a specific subject

⇐ Zach Parise

CHAPTER 1

RACKING UP
THE STATS

Hockey uses a wide range of statistics to track player performance. Fantasy hockey is no different. Fantasy leagues and teams use several stat categories to keep score. These categories include goals scored, **assists**, and shots on goal. For goaltenders important categories include wins, saves, and goals allowed.

Basic Scoring

In many fantasy leagues, a player's fantasy points are simply the total of his numbers in all the stat categories. Add up the numbers for each of the following players' stats from the 2014–2015 season. Which of them was the higher fantasy scorer? Check your answer at the bottom of the page. Which one was the more valuable fantasy player?

Sidney Crosby, Pittsburgh Penguins: 28 goals, 56 assists, 237 shots on goal

John Tavares, New York Islanders: 38 goals, 48 assists, 278 shots on goal

assist—a pass that leads to a goal by a teammate

Answer: Tavares beat out Crosby 364 points to 321.

Alex Ovechkin

FANTASY POINT *EXPLOSION*
(BASIC SCORING)

Alex Ovechkin, Washington Capitals, 2014-2015 season

- 53 goals
- 28 assists
- 395 shots on goal

Total Fantasy Points = 476

Advanced Scoring

Some fantasy hockey leagues use more advanced scoring. They award bonus points, fractional points, and even negative points, depending on the category. For example, players might get half a point for each shot on goal. They may also get bonus points for scoring on a power play. Check out the scoring chart for a common advanced scoring system.

ADVANCED FANTASY SCORING	
Goal	3 points
Assist	2 points
Power-play goal/assist	1 bonus point
Short-handed goal/assist	2 bonus points
Plus	1 point
Minus	-1 point
Shot on goal	0.5 points

Let's say that Chicago Blackhawks center Jonathan Toews had a big week for your team. In three games, he scored two goals, recorded three assists, and had 14 shots on goal. But let's dig a little deeper. One of his goals was scored during a power play. One of his assists came on a short-handed goal. Toews also had a **plus-minus** stat of plus 4 that week. Based on the above scoring system, how many points did Toews score for you? Check your answer on the next page.

2 goals, 1 on a power play $(2 \times 3) + 1 = 7$
3 assists, 1 short-handed $(3 \times 2) + 2 = 8$
14 shots $(14 \times 0.5) = 7$
Plus-4 $= 4$

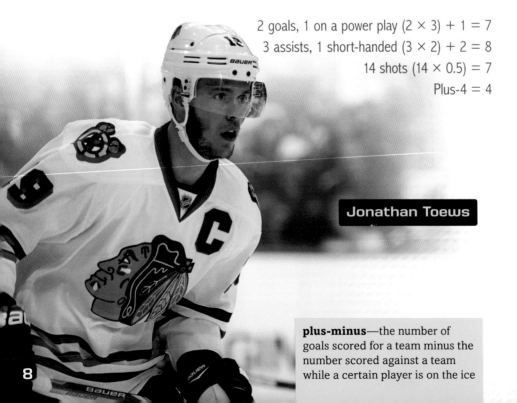

Jonathan Toews

plus-minus—the number of goals scored for a team minus the number scored against a team while a certain player is on the ice

Sam Gagner

FANTASY POINT *EXPLOSION*
(ADVANCED SCORING)

Sam Gagner, Edmonton Oilers,
February 2, 2012

    4 goals
    4 assists
    6 shots on goal
    plus-6

Total Fantasy Points = 29

Answer: 7 + 8 + 7 + 4 = 26 fantasy points

Carey Price

Between the Posts

Goaltenders are the last line of defense in pro hockey. Their job is to stop pucks and keep the other team from scoring. But goalies have a different role in fantasy hockey. They score points for your team like the skaters do. However, different stats and points are used to track a goalie's fantasy performance. The scoring chart shows basic stat categories and fantasy points used for goalies.

GOALIE STATS	POINTS
Win	4 points
Goal allowed	-1 point
Goalie save	0.25 points
Shutout	2 bonus points

Many category-based leagues also track goalies' save percentage (SV%) and goals-against average (GAA). Save percentage is figured out by dividing a goalie's saves by the total shots he faced. Let's say that Montreal Canadiens' goalie Carey Price faced 95 shots during three games. He allowed six goals. What would be his save percentage?

First, find out how many saves he made: 95 shots - 6 goals = 89 saves.
Next, divide his saves by the number of shots: $89 \div 95 = .937$ SV%

Goals-against average is a little trickier. You first multiply the number of goals allowed by 60 minutes (the length of a regulation game). Then you divide that number by the number of minutes the goalie played. Based on that, what was Price's goals-against average?

6 goals allowed × 60 minutes = 360
3 games × 50 minutes played = 150 minutes played
360 ÷ 180 = 2.4 GAA

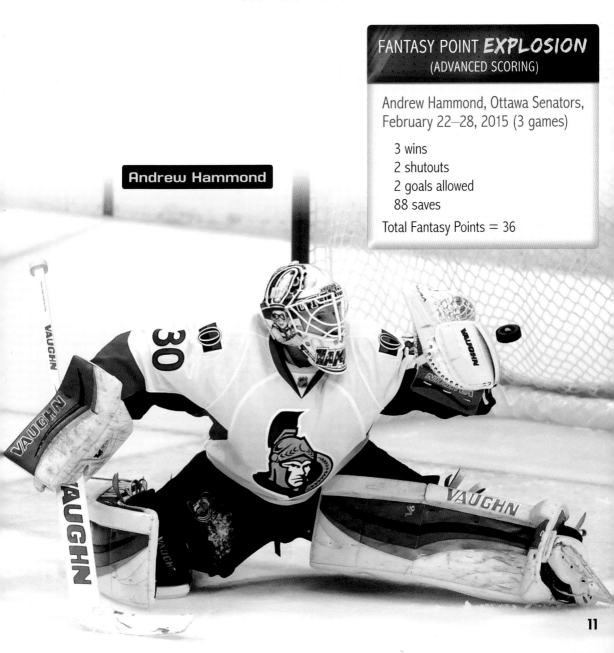

FANTASY POINT EXPLOSION
(ADVANCED SCORING)

Andrew Hammond, Ottawa Senators, February 22–28, 2015 (3 games)

3 wins
2 shutouts
2 goals allowed
88 saves
Total Fantasy Points = 36

Andrew Hammond

CHAPTER 2

PICK YOUR LEAGUE

The NHL has a long season. Teams play 82 games between October and April. In fantasy hockey, leagues often divide the season into weekly games with teams playing head-to-head (H2H). Stats from the **scoring period** are used to determine a winner. However, different types of leagues use the stats in different ways.

Head-to-Head, Points Leagues

In points-based H2H leagues, teams score points based on their players' performance. Add up the results of the following matchup between Big Al's Warriors and Mike's Mashers. In this case categories include goals scored (G), assists (A), shots on goal (SOG), wins (W), saves (SV), and goals allowed (GA). Use the advanced scoring rules explained earlier for skaters and goalies to figure out the fantasy points for each team. Which team gets the win? See if you got the correct answer on the next page.

	G	A	SOG	W	S	GA
Big Al's Warriors	16	18	62	4	120	12
Mike's Mashers	14	15	70	2	140	16

FANTASY FACT

NHL teams play three forwards (a center, a left wing, and a right wing), two defensemen, and a goaltender. Fantasy teams typically start two centers, two left wings, two right wings, four defensemen, and two goaltenders.

scoring period—the length of time that stats are totaled in a head-to-head match; scoring periods usually cover one week's worth of pro games

FANTASY POINT *EXPLOSION*
(ADVANCED SCORING)

Wayne Gretzky, Edmonton Oilers, 1985-86 season

52 goals
163 assists
11 power-play goals
3 short-handed goals
350 shots on goal
plus-71

Total Fantasy Points = 745

Wayne Gretzky

David Backes ⇑

Head-to-Head, Category Leagues

H2H leagues often keep score using categories instead of points. Point values aren't given for statistics. Instead, stats from your team are simply added up. Then the team with the best numbers in the most categories wins that week's game. Let's go back to that same game from earlier. Which team won the most categories? Look at the bottom of the page to see if you got the right answer.

	G	A	SOG	W	SV	GA
Big Al's Warriors	16	18	62	4	120	12
Mike's Mashers	14	15	70	2	140	16

FANTASY POINT *EXPLOSION*
(ADVANCED SCORING)

David Backes, St. Louis Blues, March 23-29, 2014 (4 games)

4 goals
3 assists
12 shots on goal
plus-5

Total Fantasy Points = 29

Answer: Big Al's Warriors win again, 4-2! They beat the Mashers in goals, assists, wins, and goals allowed. (Hint: for goals allowed, the lower number is better.)

Johan Franzen ⇒

Roto Rules

If you're a diehard hockey fan, you might enjoy running a team built for the long haul. A rotisserie, or roto, league might be a better fit for you. In roto leagues there are no weekly games between opponents. Fantasy teams instead rack up stats during the entire NHL season. At the end of the season, teams are ranked from first to last in each stat category. Points are then awarded based on the final rankings.

For example, in a 10-team roto league the team ranked first in each category gets 10 points. The next highest team gets 9, and so on. The nice thing about roto leagues is that you don't need to win every category to win the title. But you'll want to be near the top in each.

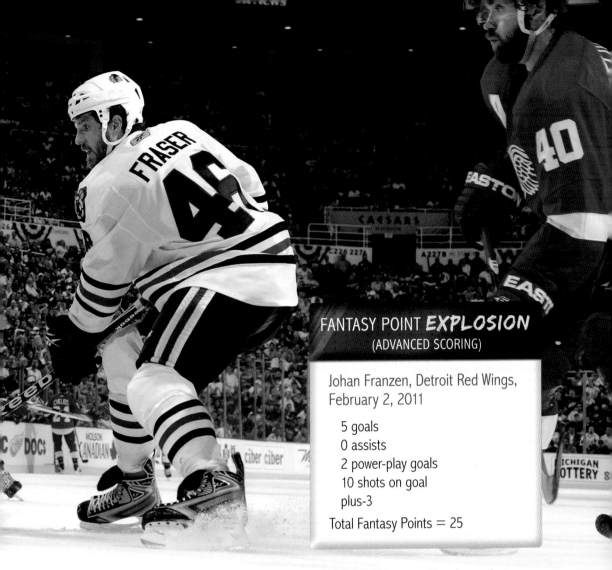

FANTASY POINT *EXPLOSION*
(ADVANCED SCORING)

Johan Franzen, Detroit Red Wings,
February 2, 2011

5 goals
0 assists
2 power-play goals
10 shots on goal
plus-3
Total Fantasy Points = 25

Take a look at the following small roto league. Rank each team from 1 to 5 in each category. The top team in each category gets five points and the bottom team gets one. Then add up each team's points to get the final scores. Check your answers in the box to see if you got the correct top-scoring team.

TEAM	G	A	W
Slap Shots	280 (1)	300 (4)	81 (4)
Ice Eagles	312 (4)	211 (1)	55 (1)
Penalty Boxers	311 (3)	390 (5)	66 (2)
Super Pucks	290 (2)	299 (3)	79 (3)
The Goons	340 (5)	280 (2)	83 (5)

Answer:
1. The Goons (12 points)
2. Penalty Boxers (10 points)
3. Slap Shots (9 points)
4. Super Pucks (8 points)
5. Ice Eagles (6 points)

17

CHAPTER 3

DRAFTING A CHAMPION

It's draft day! It's the most exciting and important day of the fantasy season. It's time to put your knowledge to work and build a winning team. With the right strategy and mix of players, you can make a run at the league championship.

Snake Drafts

Various leagues use different kinds of drafts. The most common is a snake draft, which is done in rounds. Owners take turns picking players until their **rosters** are full. The draft order is reversed in each round. If you have the first pick in Round 1, you'll get the last pick in Round 2. In a snake draft, the first two rounds usually look like the below chart.

ROUND	TEAM 1	TEAM 2	TEAM 3	TEAM 4	TEAM 5	TEAM 6	TEAM 7	TEAM 8	TEAM 9	TEAM 10
1	Pick 1	Pick 2	Pick 3	Pick 4	Pick 5	Pick 6	Pick 7	Pick 8	Pick 9	Pick 10
2	Pick 20	Pick 19	Pick 18	Pick 17	Pick 16	Pick 15	Pick 14	Pick 13	Pick 12	Pick 11

Everybody wants the Number 1 overall pick. But only one person can get the best fantasy player in the NHL. What if you're in a 10-team league and you pick last in the first round? You're actually in a pretty good spot. You'll get the first pick in round 2, meaning you can get two star players. Check out the following pairs of players and where they were drafted for the 2014-2015 season. Using basic scoring, which pair ended up being more valuable to their fantasy team? Check your answer on the next page.

⇑ Sidney Crosby

PICK #	PLAYER	G	A	SOG
1	Sidney Crosby, Pittsburgh Penguins	28	56	237
20	Taylor Hall, Edmonton Oilers	14	24	158

PICK #	PLAYER	G	A	SOG
10	Jamie Benn, Dallas Stars	35	52	253
11	Patrick Kane, Chicago Blackhawks	27	37	186

roster—a list of players on a team

Answer: Benn and Kane were the better fantasy pair. They outscored Crosby and Hall, 590–517.

Going Once, Going Twice, Sold!

If you owned a real hockey team, you'd have to decide how much money you can pay your players. You'd also have to make sure to stay under the **salary cap**.

Auction drafts work the same way. In an auction draft team owners are given a certain amount of imaginary money. They take turns bidding on the players they want. Players are awarded to the highest bidders. This can be a fun and challenging way to build a team. However, you have to stay within your **budget**. If you have $200 and need to fill a 16-player roster, what's the average amount you can spend on each player? Look below to see if your answer is right.

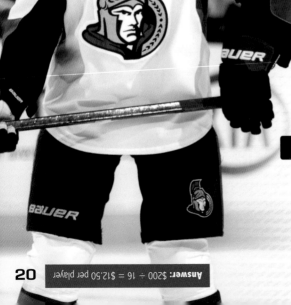

Erik Karlsson

Of course, you won't spend the same amount on each player. You can throw big money at star players. But you need to be careful. Let's say you manage to grab the Ottawa Senators' Erik Karlsson for $60 and drop $50 on Nashville Predators goalie Pekka Rinne. You've got a couple of great stars. But now you have just $90 left for the rest of your team. What is the average amount you can spend on the remaining players? Look on the next page for the correct answer.

salary cap—a limit of the total amount of money that can be spent on a team's players

budget—a plan for how to spend a fixed amount of money effectively

Answer: $200 ÷ 16 = $12.50 per player

⇐ Pekka Rinne

FINDERS KEEPERS

If you really love your players, you might want to try a dynasty or keeper league. These leagues allow owners to hang onto one or more players year after year. But you need to think carefully about which players to keep. Consider factors such as a player's age and how long you think he'll continue to perform. Pick the right players and you can dominate your league for years. But pick the wrong ones and you'll be watching another owner claim the championship.

CHAPTER 4

KEEPING YOUR TEAM
COMPETITIVE

You've drafted your team, and you like what you see. But you can't just sit back and relax. You're not just the team owner. You're a manager too. You need to choose the best starting lineup each week. You'll likely also need to make some **transactions** during the season to keep your team in the hunt for the title.

Setting Your Starters

Oh no! It's just five weeks into the season. Your star center, Tampa Bay Lightning center Steven Stamkos, has broken his leg. Luckily, you have the Ottawa Senators' Kyle Turris and the St. Louis Blues' Paul Stastny stashed on your bench. But which of these centers should you start in Stamkos' place? Take a look at their average points over the first five weeks to help you decide.

	G	A	SOG	FANTASY POINTS	AVG POINTS/GAME
Stastny	6	7	28	46	9.2
Turris	4	14	49	44.5	8.9

Stastny has the lead. But it's close. He has more goals, but Turris has more shots on goal. He takes a lot more shots, which could lead to more goals during the season. Either player could net you points. But it might be worth taking a gamble on Turris.

transaction—a change on a team's roster, such as dropping or adding players, or making a trade

Paul Stastny ⇓

Combing the Waiver Wire

As the season goes on, you'll notice some undrafted players will start to shine. They may even be out-performing your guys. It might be time to check out the **waiver wire**. It's often a good idea to grab a hot **free agent** or two to help strengthen your team.

Perhaps your team could use some goaltending help. Say that the Minnesota Wild's Devan Dubnyk is red-hot right now and happens to be available. Is he better than the goalies on your roster? Compare their stats to see if Dubnyk is worth adding to your team.

FREE AGENT	WINS	SHUTOUTS	SV%	GA
Devan Dubnyk, Minnesota Wild	10	4	.938	1.54

YOUR GOALIES				
Corey Crawford, Chicago Blackhawks	6	0	.918	2.55
Ryan Miller, Vancouver Canucks	6	3	.914	2.25
Brian Elliott, St. Louis Blues	7	1	.919	2.30

waiver wire—a list of available players in a fantasy sports league

free agent—a player who is not on another team

Based on the stats, adding Dubnyk is a no-brainer. But who do you drop to get him? Do you dare let Corey Crawford go? He's had the least success, but he's been solid in the past. There's no right or wrong answer here. You'll need to evaluate each goalie's performance and decide which of them are best to keep on your team.

Devan Dubnyk

Dustin Byfuglien

Swap Meet

Another way to upgrade your team is through wheeling and dealing your players with trades. Trading players is no easy task. You'll likely have to give up something to get something. The trick is finding willing trade partners who also want to upgrade their teams.

How do you improve your team without weakening it? Perhaps you have a strong group of defensemen. You might have a player riding your bench who could start for another team. Can you dangle him out there and hope to get a strong forward in return? Check out this **blockbuster trade** involving several star players. Would your team be stronger if you made this deal?

YOU GIVE UP	AVG FANTASY POINTS/WEEK
Dustin Byfuglien, D, Winnipeg Jets	9.5
Jonathan Quick, G, Los Angeles Kings	14.9

YOU GET IN RETURN	
Claude Giroux, RW, Philadelphia Flyers	14.8
Jaromir Jagr, RW, Florida Panthers	9.0

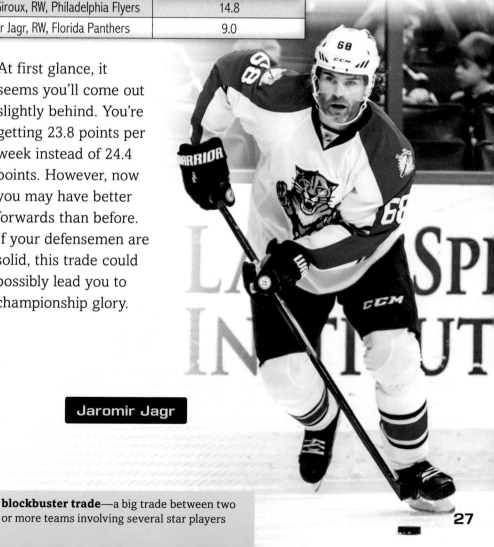

At first glance, it seems you'll come out slightly behind. You're getting 23.8 points per week instead of 24.4 points. However, now you may have better forwards than before. If your defensemen are solid, this trade could possibly lead you to championship glory.

Jaromir Jagr

blockbuster trade—a big trade between two or more teams involving several star players

Let's Play Hockey!

Pro hockey is an exciting sport full of fast skating, bone-crushing hits, and sweet goals. On its own, the sport can be thrilling to watch. But for fantasy players, it can provide an extra level of excitement and drama.

To be a successful fantasy hockey owner, you don't need to be a world-class athlete. You just need to be smart about the numbers. Being able to crunch the stats will help your team find success. Once you learn to do the math, you can soon begin to dominate your league. Before you know it, you'll be hoisting the league trophy and basking in fantasy hockey glory!

GLOSSARY

assist (uh-SIST)—a pass that leads to a goal by a teammate

blockbuster trade (BLOK-bus-tuhr TRAYD)—a big trade between two or more teams involving several star players

budget (BUH-juht)—a plan for how to spend a fixed amount of money effectively

free agent (FREE AYJ-uhnt)—a player who is not on another team

hat trick (HAT TRIK)—when a hockey player scores three goals in a single game

plus-minus (PLUS MY-nuhs)—the number of goals scored for a team minus the number of goals scored against a team while a certain player is on the ice

roster (ROS-tur)—a list of players on a team

salary cap (SAL-uh-ree KAP)—a limit of the total amount of money that can be spent on a team's players

scoring period (SKOR-ing PEER-ee-uhd)—the length of time that stats are totaled in a head-to-head match; scoring periods usually cover one week's worth of pro games

statistics (stuh-TISS-tiks)—numbers, facts, or other data collected about a specific subject

transaction (tran-ZAK-shuhn)—a change on a team's roster, such as adding or dropping a player, or making a trade

waiver wire (WAYV-uhr WIRE)—a list of available players in a sports league

READ MORE

Frederick, Shane. *Hockey Stats and the Stories Behind Them: What Every Fan Needs to Know.* Sports Stats and Stories. North Mankato, Minn.: Capstone Press, 2016.

Kortemeier, Todd. *Pro Hockey by the Numbers.* Pro Sports by the Numbers. North Mankato, Minn.: Capstone Press, 2016.

Robinson, Tom. *Hockey: Math at the Rink.* Math in Sports. Mankato, Minn.: Child's World, 2013.

INTERNET SITES

FactHound offers a safe, fun way to find Internet sites related to this book. All of the sites on FactHound have been researched by our staff.

Here's all you do:

Visit *www.facthound.com*

Type in this code: 9781515721727

 Check out projects, games and lots more at
www.capstonekids.com

INDEX